NEW
EMPLOYEE
INDUCTION

Better Management Skills

This highly popular range of inexpensive paperbacks covers all areas of basic management. Practical, easy to read and instantly accessible, these guides will help managers to improve their business or communication skills. Those marked * are available on audio cassette.

The books in this series can be tailored to specific company requirements. For further details, please contact the publisher, Kogan Page, telephone 0171 278 0433, fax 0171 837 6348.

Be a Successful Supervisor
Be Positive
Building High Performance Teams
Business Creativity
Business Ethics
Business Etiquette
Coaching Your Employees
Conducting Effective Interviews
Counselling Your Staff
Creating a Learning Organisation
Creative Decision-making
Creative Thinking in Business
Delegating for Results
Develop Your Assertiveness
Effective Business Briefings
Effective Employee Participation
Effective Meeting Skills
Effective Networking for
   Professional Success
Effective Performance Appraisals*
Effective Presentation Skills
Empowering People
Empowerment
Facilitation Skills for Team
   Development
First Time Supervisor
Get Organised!
Goals and Goal Setting
How to Communicate Effectively*
How to Develop a Positive
   Attitude*
How to Manage Organisational Change
How to Motivate People*
How to Plan Your Competitive
   Strategy
How to Reward Your Staff
How to Understand Financial
   Statements
How to Write a Marketing Plan
How to Write a Staff Manual

Improving Relations at Work
Keeping Customers for Life
Leadership Skills for Women
Learning to Lead
Making TQM Work
Managing Cultural Diversity at Work
Managing Disagreement
   Constructively
Managing Employee Stress
Managing Organisational
   Change
Managing Part-time Employees
Managing Quality Customer
   Service
Managing Your Boss
Marketing for Success
Memory Skills in Business
Mentoring
NLP for Business Success
Office Management
Organisation Design
Personnel Testing
Process Improvement
Project Management from
   Idea to Implementation
Quality Customer Service for
   Front Line Staff
Rate Your Skills as a Manager
Sales Training Basics
Self-managing Teams
Selling Professionally
Successful Negotiation
Successful Presentation Skills
Successful Telephone Techniques
Systematic Problem-solving and
   Decision-making
Team Building
Training Methods that Work
The Internal Consultant
The Woman Manager

NEW
EMPLOYEE
INDUCTION

A PRACTICAL GUIDE
TO IMPLEMENTING
AN EFFECTIVE PROGRAMME

CHARLES M CADWELL

KOGAN PAGE
BETTER MANAGEMENT SKILLS

First published in the United States of America in 1997, entitled *New Employee Orientation*, by Crisp Publications Inc, 1200 Hamilton Court, Menlo Park, California 94025, USA.

This edition first published in Great Britain in 1998 by Kogan Page Ltd, 120 Pentonville Road, London N1 9JN.

British Library Cataloguing in Publication Data

A CIP record for this book is available from the British Library.

ISBN 0-7494-2718-3

Typeset by BookEns Ltd, Royston, Herts.
Printed in England by Clays Ltd, St Ives plc

Contents

Preface

This book will provide specific guidelines on how to conduct new employee induction for any manager or supervisor. *New Employee Induction* is not a guide about how to develop an employee handbook. There are several books available which can help you do that. Very few books, however, tell you how to conduct a logical, positive new employee induction programme. Too many organizations feel that giving a good company handbook to a new employee is a sufficient induction. Although having an employee handbook is an *important* part of an effective induction process, it is not a substitute for conducting a personal induction.

Companies spend considerable money recruiting, interviewing and often relocating new employees. Then, once a hiring decision has been made and the new employee arrives for work, most organizations provide very little formal attention to reinforce the employee's (often difficult) decision to accept the new position.

The guidelines provided in this book, if applied, will help a new employee feel welcome, learn the basics more quickly and become productive much sooner.

To the Reader

New Employee Induction is not like most books. It's not a book to read, it's a book to use. The unique 'self-paced' format of this book, and the many worksheets, encourage the reader to get involved and develop some new approaches to new employee induction.

New Employee Induction can be used effectively in a number of ways. Here are some possibilities:

- *Self-study.* Because the book is self-instructional, all that is needed is a quiet place and some time. By completing the activities and exercises, a reader should not only receive valuable feedback, but also practical ideas about what to do when he or she has a new employee.
- *Workshops and seminars.* The book is ideal for assigned reading prior to a workshop or seminar. With the basics in hand, the quality of the participation will improve, and more time can be spent on application during the programme. The book is also effective when it is distributed at the beginning of a session, and participants 'work through' the contents.
- *Remote location training.* Books can be sent to those not able to attend 'home office' training sessions.

There are several other possibilities that depend on the objectives, programme or ideas of the user.

One thing is for sure, even after it has been read this book will be looked at — and thought about — again and again.

Introduction

On average, 17 per cent of the working population leave their job per annum. This means that, potentially, one in six employees faces a first day in a new job every year.

One reason people change jobs is that they never feel welcome or a part of the organization they join. As a result, many choose to switch, rather than fight, and simply quit their jobs and move on to another company shortly after they are hired. When this happens, the organization they leave behind is faced once again with the need to hire, induct and train another employee. The cost of doing this has been estimated to be anywhere from £37,000 to £22,000 *per person*, depending on the position in the organization.

A thoughtful new employee induction programme can reduce turnover and save an organization thousands of dollars. Whether a company has two employees or 20,000, it should not leave new employee induction to chance.

More and more organizations are beginning to realize the positive benefits of utilizing part-time workers. Unfortunately they often think of these employees as not needing induction, since they will only be there for a short while. This attitude often contributes to an even higher turnover rate.

New Employee Induction outlines specific steps organizations can take to reduce both permanent and part-time employee turnover and at the same time quickly prepare workers for their new jobs. Reduced turnover along with better inducted and trained employees means better service for the customer.

In today's service-oriented economy a significant advantage can be provided to the company that used the methods described in this book.

Just as you must develop a logical, thoughtful plan to start a successful business, you also need to take the same approach when inducting new employees.

If you apply the principles outlined in this book, you will learn how to:

- evaluate your current induction programme
- begin your induction during the interview process
- develop a plan for successful induction
- induct both permanent and part-time employees.

Remember, when employees succeed, the organization succeeds. A thorough, well-planned induction is a first step on that road to success.

CHAPTER 1
The Benefits of Proper Induction

Objectives

Objectives give us a sense of direction and purpose. They define what we want to accomplish and provide a way to measure our success. Objectives are a road-map that takes us from where we are to where we want to be.

An effective new employee induction programme will accomplish the following objectives:

- provide a genuine welcome
- develop positive perceptions about the organization
- confirm the employee's decision to join the organization
- teach basic fundamentals each new employee should know
- provide a basis for training
- put the employee at ease.

In addition to these objectives, I want to:

_____

_____

_____

_____

Are you meeting your objectives?

Think for a moment about the last few people your organization employed, then honestly answer the questions below (circle either Y (yes) or N (no)).

	Employee 1		Employee 2		Employee 3	
Name:						
1. How long has each employee been on board?						
2. Do you think the employee was made to feel welcome?	Y	N	Y	N	Y	N
3. Do you think the employee regrets his or her decision to join your organization?	Y	N	Y	N	Y	N
4. Was the employee productive within a short period of time?	Y	N	Y	N	Y	N
5. Did your organization have a planned induction programme?	Y	N	Y	N	Y	N
6. If you had been in the employee's place, would you have been satisfied with the induction?	Y	N	Y	N	Y	N

Circle the number that best describes the induction these employees received.

1	2	3	4	5
Poor	Needs improvement	Not sure	Good	The best

Why a planned induction pays dividends

Most new employees arrive for the first day of work full of enthusiasm and excitement. This initial interest can either be put to positive use, or destroyed, depending on how it is nurtured.

New employee induction is not difficult and need not consume a large amount of time. In fact, when done properly, induction will save time in the long run.

A poorly planned or non-existent induction can quickly turn a carefully recruited and selected employee into another turnover statistic. If this occurs, it means more work for your organization because it will be necessary to start the entire employment process over.

A well-planned and executed induction, on the other hand, will result in fewer mistakes and a better understanding of what is expected. This should lead to improved customer service, higher productivity and improved employee relations. Everyone wins – you, the employee, the organization, and most of all, your customers or clients.

The goal of induction is to capitalize on each new employee's enthusiasm and keep it alive once the work begins. When induction is successful, a new employee will become a valued asset to the organization.

Larger organizations are constantly employing, inducting and training new employees. Many do it because they require seasonal help (ie, Christmas, Easter, summer, etc) during peak business periods. Other do it because of their reliance on inexperienced workers (ie, fast food outlets, convenience stores, etc). These workers change jobs frequently for a variety of reasons.

A well-organized induction can especially benefit organizations that need to induct large numbers of employees in short periods of time. Chapter 4 of this book deals with specific things these organizations can do to develop a quality induction programme.

The balance of this first section will examine specific things any organization can do to meet the goals and objectives of new employee induction.

To begin, it would be a good idea to review your own induction. Often, we tend to imitate what we have experienced. If you received a good induction, it is likely you will remember to pass along some of the items you experienced. If your induction was poor, or lacking, this book can help you develop a positive programme. Either way, by completing the exercises in the pages that follow, you will better prepared to make new employees more productive and happier as they begin their careers.

(The following page asks you to evaluate the induction you received.)

How did your induction rate?

Think back to when you started your current job. Read each statement and circle either T (true) or F (false) as it relates to the induction you received. Then check your rating in the box following this questionnaire.

1. I was made to feel welcome   T   F
2. I was introduced to other members of my work group.   T   F
3. My boss paid attention to me and made me feel welcome.   T   F
4. My induction seemed well planned.   T   F
5. Company benefits were well explained the first day.   T   F
6. My office or work space was set up and waiting for me.   T   F
7. I received a tour of the organization by a qualified person.   T   F
8. All the necessary paperwork and forms were available, and I received assistance in completing them properly.   T   F
9. I received a copy of relevant literature, such as the company's Employee Handbook, Operations Manual, etc.   T   F
10. I learnt about the company's history and future plans.   T   F
11. My boss reviewed my formal job description with me.   T   F
12. I was invited to lunch the first day by my boss or a key individual he or she selected.   T   F
13. I met people from other departments.   T   F

14. I was able to observe colleagues at work before starting
    a task.   T F
15. I was given a specific job assignment along with
    instruction or training.   T F
16. Office hours, dress code, sick leave and other policies
    were explained to me.   T F
17. I was shown the phone system.   T F
18. I had opportunities to ask questions.   T F
19. Payroll policies (and withholding) were covered my
    first day.   T F
20. At the end of the first week I felt like a member of
    the 'team'.   T F

Total number true: _____ false: _____

18–20 true: Your induction was outstanding, I hope it was
            appreciated.
15–17 true: Your induction was above average. You are in a
            position to make some improvements.
11–14 true: Unfortunately you received a typical induction.
            There is a lot you can do to help your organization
            with future induction.
10 or less: You should be congratulated for sticking it out.
            Don't let the same thing happen to others.

Provide a welcome

You never get a second chance to make a good first
impression. Induction is the time to roll out the red carpet.
This simple act is often overlooked when a new employee
arrives for work.

Why is it that most organizations hold elaborate 'going
away' parties when an employee leaves (often to a
competitor)? It suggests that leaving is a cause for celebration.

Wouldn't it be better to have a celebration when a new
employee arrives? Why not have a party in the beginning to
let the new employee get acquainted.

An easy way to provide such a welcome is to designate a

room and time (usually an hour will be sufficient) to invite selected employees to meet the new person. Coffee and biscuits add a nice touch.

This will make the new employee the centre of attention at the beginning and provide an opportunity to meet key people in a relaxed, informal setting.

All members of the new employee's 'team' should be encouraged to attend the gathering. They should be coached to go out of their way to make the new employee feel welcome. Nothing is worse then an insincere gathering where 'veterans' talk with each other and exclude the newcomer. If this happens, it is better to postpone this event until everyone understands their roles.

Another way to make an employee feel welcome is to publicize the employer's decision. An announcement memo should be sent to all appropriate individuals or an article should be developed for the company newsletter. Information about the employee's background, family and specific job responsibilities is usually a good idea.

Most local newspapers have business sections that print information about promotions and new employees. Send or phone information to them when appropriate. For special employees, you might consider a press release with a photo to use with the story.

Making a new employee feel welcome is easy if you do some planning. The worksheet below will help you plan your welcome.

Planning worksheet – providing a welcome

List the items that need to be planned the next time you conduct a new employee induction.

Welcoming event:_____

_____

_____

Publicity: _____

_____

_____

Other ideas: _____

_____

_____

Information checklist — have you included?

- full name
- photo (if appropriate)
- specific job title
- immediate manager
- special assignments
- other
- previous work experience
- education (if appropriate)
- effective start date
- spouse's name (if appropriate)
- children and ages (if appropriate)
- hobbies, other interests

Develop positive perceptions

Induction is a critical time. This is when a new employee develops perceptions about the organization, other employees and you as a supervisor or manager.

It is critical to make a positive impression during this period. A planned and organized induction will communicate that you are in control of the situation and the organization has definite quality standards.

New employees are naturally observant of the environment. They notice how well things are organized, whether a businesslike atmosphere exists and whether it will be an enjoyable place to work. This initial opinion, once formed, can be hard to change. It is, therefore, essential that you do everything possible to create a positive perception.

When the new employee sees the real company, it should be the same one he or she saw during the recruiting and interviewing process. If this is not the case, the new employee will reconsider if this is the atmosphere in which he or she wants to work. Many new employees change their minds quickly without giving an organization the full benefit of their consideration because the job seems different from the one they expected. These expectations are usually based on perceptions generated during the interview.

Everything that happens the first few days will affect a new employee's perceptions and these will be passed on to friends, family and colleagues at the previous job. They will hear both the good and the bad. The quality of the induction, therefore, is a reflection of an organization as much as any product or service that is offered.

Perceptions are especially important to part-time workers. These employees understand that if the job doesn't measure up they can move on to another organization.

You create positive perceptions by being organized and having a planned induction

What perception do you create?

Perceptions are made up of many factors. This questionnaire will help you evaluate the perceptions you create.

Circle Y (yes) or N (no) depending on which best describes what a person would observe when visiting your work area.

1. Our work area is neat and organized.   Y   N
2. If a specific file is needed, it can be easily located.   Y   N
3. The whereabouts of all employees is known.   Y   N
4. When supervisors are out of the office, normal
   work continues.   Y   N

5. Employees are busy and appear to be doing productive work.   Y   N
6. Our employees are friendly and outgoing.   Y   N
7. Job applicants would receive an accurate picture of what our organization is like is they observed our work area for a while.   Y   N
8. My family and friends think I work for a great organization.   Y   N
9. I say positive things about our operation to others.   Y   N
10. We can describe our new employee induction programme to job candidates.   Y   N

Total number yes: _____ no: _____

If you answered 'yes' to:

9–10: Excellent. You create a positive perception.
7–8: The perceptions you create are generally positive, but some improvement is possible.
5–6: You are sending out a negative message. Get to work.
4 or less: Time to take a hard look at the perception you are creating. Things won't improve until you begin making some basic changes.

CASE STUDY
Marge Jackson develops new perceptions

Marge Jackson waited in the reception area with great anticipation. She finally had been asked to interview for an administrative assistant position with Alpha-Omega Business Systems. She had heard it was a great place to work. She sent her resumé in three months ago, but hadn't heard anything until two days ago. Although her interview with Sam Wilson wasn't scheduled to start until 11.30 am, she decided to get there 15 minutes early to make a good impression.

During her wait she observed several things about the company. The receptionist, Miss Parker, had greeted her warmly and offered her a cup of coffee. A few minutes later an employee, who was looking for a file, asked Miss Parker to help him. There was a discussion, some of it obviously toned down because of Marge's presence, which resulted in the employee storming out of the office. A few minutes later Miss Parker took a phone call and explained to the caller that Mr Miller just left and she didn't know when he would return.

Just as she hung up another employee approached Miss Parker and the two began discussing last night's TV shows. When their discussion was finished, the employee came over to Marge and introduced herself as Jan Lock. She told Marge that she would really like working at Alpha-Omega, because the atmosphere was very relaxed and no one minded if you were a little bit late in the morning or left early in the afternoon.

At 11.45 am Mr Wilson appeared at Miss Parker's desk and asked if there were any messages for him. Miss Parker explained that Marge had been waiting for an interview for the administrative assistant position since 11.30 am.

Mr Wilson looked surprised. After a few seconds he walked over to Marge and explained that the position had been filled earlier that morning. He said he was sorry she had not been notified and hoped that she would keep Alpha-Omega in mind in the future.

What positive perceptions were created for Marge by Alpha-Omega?

_____

_____

_____

_____

What negative perceptions were created for Marge by Alpha-Omega?

_____

_____

_____

_____

How could Alpha-Omega improve the perceptions they create?

_____

_____

_____

_____

What type of induction do you think Marge Jackson would have received if she had been hired by Alpha-Omega?

_____

_____

_____

_____

Self-assessment

The following statements summarize key points presented in this chapter. Check those that are true most of the time for you and your organization. Review all items not checked in order to improve future inductions.

- New employees remain enthusiastic after being on the job several months. ☐
- New employee turnover is lower now than it was six months ago. ☐
- I routinely take time to get to know my employees. ☐
- Our company has an employee handbook that is kept up to date. ☐
- All managers and supervisors have a plan for inducting new employees. ☐

- Welcoming events are scheduled to help new employees get acquainted. ☐
- Publicity about a new employee is routinely circulated. ☐
- We create positive perceptions by keeping things organized. ☐
- Our company has a reputation for being a great place to work. ☐
- New employees have the opportunity to ask questions when they don't understand something. ☐

Areas where improvement is needed:

_____

_____

_____

You can probably think of situations in which what you expected and what actually happened were totally different. You may have left (or at least considered leaving) a job because of the poor induction you received.

New employee induction must be planned. New employees are willing and eager to learn. If you don't have a plan to use their enthusiasm you can quickly dampen their spirits. Don't let that happen. Get them started right and you'll increase the chance of developing a positive, long-term working relationship.

CHAPTER 2
Planning for Success

Introduction

When you plan for success, you are more likely to achieve it. This chapter will discuss the factors you can use to your advantage when planning a new employee induction programme.

Confirm job decision

Induction is a great way to allow the new employee to confirm that he or she has made the right employment choice. An employee will be looking for assurance from you to reinforce the decision of choosing your company as the place to work.

It is likely that your new employee was interviewed by other organizations. Since you felt the person was a good choice, others may have also. The decision to select your organization may have been a difficult one, so the first day is a perfect time to reinforce the employee's decision to work for you.

How many times have you seen (or heard about) a new employee leaving a new job within a few weeks? It is not uncommon. Usually the reason given is, 'This wasn't what I expected'. Most turnover of this type occurs during the first month. This is especially true of businesses that employ hourly workers. Chapter 4 discusses the special problems of induction in high turnover environments. If the employee survives the first month, the chances of a long-term relationship are improved. You will significantly increase the chances of keeping a new employee when an induction plan clearly spells out you expectations.

The initial expectations that are communicated have a decided impact on an employee's job performance. If you expect quality performance and communicate it by both word and deed, you increase the probability of getting high performance. On the other hand, if you communicate low expectations, that's what you're likely to receive.

You control a new employee's expectations. If you developed expectations during the recruiting process that are not realistic, you will soon find yourself with the same job opening. Keep in mind that every interaction you have with a potential employee communicates expectations and sets an example.

Were your expectations met?

Think back to when you started your current job. How well did your company meet your expectations for each item listed?

- Exceeded expectation   5
- Met expectations   4
- Partially met expectations 3
- Left a lot to be desired   2
- Missed completely   1

1. Introductions to others   ____
2. Tour of the workplace   ____
3. Friendliness of co-workers   ____
4. Helpfulness of supervisor/manager   ____
5. Organized work area   ____
6. First job assignment   ____
7. Explanation of how things work   ____
8. Help in relocating (if applicable)   ____

9. Explanation of benefits   ____

10. Planned induction   ____

Note any item that you rated as 3 or less. These are areas you need to plan in advance in order to meet the expectations of your new employees. For those items you rated as 4 or 5, be sure to continue the positive approach that you received.

Define your expectations

One induction goal is to help the employee confirm that he or she made the right decision to work for you.

In the last section you evaluated how well your expectations were met. How about you expectations for those you hire? Answer the questions below to help clarify your expectations for a new employee.

What specific job expectations do you have for new employees?

_____

_____

_____

How do you communicate these expectations in a positive manner during the recruiting process?

_____

_____

_____

How do you communicate your expectations the first day?

_____

_____

_____

How do you communicate your expectations the first week?

_____

_____

_____

Set the stage for training

Induction is the time to get the employee started on the right foot. A well-planned programme will set the stage for all training that follows. A thoughtful induction should answer most basic questions a new employee might have. When this happens, attention can be focused on teaching skills needed to perform a job.

Without a well-planned induction programme, new employees are forced to learn on their own. This can be time consuming and inefficient. Often an employee will lack some essential information or receive incorrect or misleading information. If an induction programme is lacking or poorly planned, considerable time will be wasted reinventing the wheel.

When given proper direction, a clear assignment and specific information, a new employee is more likely to get started correctly and will be more receptive when it is time to begin training.

Induction should provide a new employee with the necessary information about his or her role in the organization. This is best done in a one-on-one meeting but can be accomplished in a group session.

Putting the employee at ease on the first day

The first day in the job is filled with anxiety and uncertainty for most new employees. Almost all want to make a good first impression and do things right. In an effort to fit in, some new employees may say or do things that seem forced or brash. Others will react just the opposite. They may fear doing or saying the wrong thing and consequently won't do anything without being specifically asked or directed.

One of the best ways to keep things relaxed is to introduce everyone in a friendly, relaxed environment. The sooner a new employee gets to know his or her co-workers, the better. The earlier people know each other the better the chances of a positive long-term working relationship.

It is important to verbalize that the organization is pleased the new employee is on board. If the employee feels confident that he or she will fit in and be able to make important contributions a positive perception has been created.

It is also a good idea to reinforce that help is available if there are any questions. Take time to answer questions and provide clear direction. Do everything in your power to help the new employee succeed.

Planning the induction

In the space provided, indicate how you plan to accomplish each of the following objectives during the induction you conduct.

• Provide clear direction about job expectations

_____

_____

_____

_____

• Explain organization structure

_____

_____

_____

_____

- Make first job assignment

_____

_____

_____

_____

- Give specific background information

_____

_____

_____

_____

CASE STUDY
Susan Beal's expectations

Susan Beal, the new accounting supervisor, arrived for her first day of work at Accounting Unlimited with expectations for a great first day. As she drove to work she envisioned a day full of learning about the company, its plans for the future and the role she would play in helping the company succeed. She couldn't wait to get started.

Susan's boss, Joan Parker, met her at 8.00 am and brought Susan a cup of coffee. Joan suggested they start the day with a tour of the office. Just as they were starting, Joan's secretary came in with an urgent message. Joan's boss needed to see her right away to discuss the revised budget. Joan took Susan to meet Mark Langston, another account supervisor and one of Susan's co-workers. She asked Mark to take Susan on the tour and said she would be back shortly to continue the induction.

Mark was very busy and appeared annoyed at being interrupted. He agreed, however, to take Susan on the office tour while Joan went to the meeting with her boss. Mark's tour lasted just five minutes and included several comments about how hard it was to get things done with all the interruptions.

Mark took Susan to her new office area and told her to wait there for Joan to return. Susan waited and waited. Finally at 10.30 am Joan returned and told Susan there were problems and her meeting would last until at least noon. She handed Susan several project files and suggested Susan read through them until she returned. If Susan had any questions she was to talk to Mark.

Consider Susan Beal's situation and answer these questions:

What was positive about Susan's induction?

_____

_____

_____

What impression do you think Susan has of Accounting Unlimited?

_____

_____

_____

What impression do you think Susan has of her new boss?

_____

_____

_____

How could the situation have been avoided?

_____

_____

_____

How can Joan Parker recover from the problems of the morning?

_____

_____

_____

Summary

An effective induction should take advantage of a new employee's enthusiasm and keep it alive. As the supervisor, you have the most immediate impact on creating a positive environment. You accomplish this by developing a well-planned induction.

An effective induction should meet these objectives:

- provide a genuine welcome
- develop positive perceptions about the organization
- confirm the employee's decision to join the organization
- teach basic fundamentals each new employee should know
- provide a basis for training
- put the employee at ease.

These objectives can be achieved by using the procedures outlined in the next section. Before proceeding, however, take a few minutes to answer the situation presented in the next section. If you can answer these questions you are on your way to conducting an effective new employee induction.

Review
The next time I conduct a new employee induction, I will plan ahead as follows:

I will provide a welcome by:

_____

_____

_____

_____

I can develop positive perceptions by:

_____

_____

_____

_____

I will establish positive, realistic expectations by:

_____

_____

_____

_____

I plan to reinforce the job decision by:

_____

_____

_____

_____

I will lay the foundation for subsequent training by:

_____

_____

_____

_____

I will put the employee at ease by:

_____

_____

_____

_____

CHAPTER 3

Induction for Permanent Employees

Do it right and only do it once

Someone in your organization (maybe you) spent considerable time reviewing resumés and applications. Additional time was spent interviewing for an open decision. Then a decision had to made about the right person for the job.

Now the person that was selected for your job is ready to go to work and it is time for an induction programme. This section will help you establish or refine such a programme.

A successful induction process should be customized to fit the particular needs of an organization and a new employee. Successful programmes are carefully planned and implemented so they are done once and done right. Otherwise a poor impression is the result and productivity will suffer.

Start induction during the interview

The interview process is where induction begins. When a job is discussed with the applicant, the following items, at a minimum, should be covered:

- background of the organization
- general job description
- performance evaluation procedures

- work hours
- compensation
- holiday and time off
- benefits
- probation period.

Each of these items, plus any others you feel are pertinent, should be discussed and available in written form if the prospective employee wishes. These represent basic considerations that any applicant wants to know before making an informed decision about joining a company. By covering these points before a job offer is made, you provide a chance for the prospective employee to evaluate the job objectively.

Often an applicant may decide the job us not suitable based on the factors presented during the interview. If an applicant withdraws from consideration because of a disagreement about the job basics, you have probably come out ahead. This is far better than investing induction and training time, only to lose the new employee the first month because he or she had a problem with the terms and conditions of employment.

Start your induction during the interview process and you will save time and energy that can be devoted to employees who know what the job offers.

Consider a prospective employee kit

You can save valuable time by preparing a friendly package of documents for prospective employees. The 'kit' can be given during the interview process to help an applicant decide if he or she would be a good fit with the company.

Such a kit can be used throughout your organization by anyone who has contact with prospective employees.

If you already have a set of hand-outs for prospective employees, use the following checklist to ensure it is complete (circle Y (yes) or N (no)).

Does your prospective employee kit include:

name, address and phone number of organization	Y	N
names and titles of key executives	Y	N
a brief history of the organization	Y	N
normal working hours	Y	N
pay periods	Y	N
holiday and time-off policies	Y	N
medical and other benefits	Y	N
type of new employee probation period	Y	N
contact person following the interview	Y	N
specific job description	Y	N
specific salary information	Y	N
For out-of-town interviewees, do you have ...		
general information about the neighbourhood or city?	Y	N
address and phone number of Chamber of Commerce?	Y	N
names and numbers of several reputable estate agents?	Y	N
name of employment agencies (for spouse)?	Y	N

Note: The specific job description and salary mentioned above are provided separately from the standard kit.

Induction template

On page 69 of this book is an 'induction template'. It is provided for you to use while developing a complete induction plan. There are also several checklists to help you develop a customized plan for your organization.

Each new employee is different. Each has a specific set of skills and aptitudes. Each has a unique personality. Your induction will be more effective if you take individual differences into account. However, in addition to being sensitive to individual differences, you must also develop a standardized list of items. Your challenge, therefore, is to address an individual's needs, yet use a standardized approach to ensure all bases are covered. There are several ways to accomplish this goal.

The best induction is one that involves the employee to the fullest extent possible. If you give a new employee the opportunity to feed back what he or she most wants to learn, the prospects for an excellent induction are significantly increased.

One way to accomplish this is by asking the applicant several questions during the interview. For example, you might ask, 'What would you like to learn first?' 'What are your expectations for the first day?' 'What projects are you most interested in learning about?'

Involve the employee

Involving the new employee can also be done at the beginning of the induction by presenting a schedule of items you intend to cover and asking which are most relevant. This way the new employee knows what is planned and has an opportunity to add other items or issues. He or she will also see that you have taken time to make the induction meaningful.

Another consideration is to schedule aspects of the programme around the employee's work schedule. The person making the job assignments should stagger the induction so it will not conflict with an employee's new responsibilities. Essential information, plus that which the employee is most interested in, can be covered early and the employee will be able to cover the rest over time.

The checklists and template on pages 67 and 69 are excellent starting points. Each item on the list should determine what specific information you need to properly cover that topic with a new employee. Remember, your job is to personalize the induction process to meet the specific needs of each employee.

Induction is an ongoing process

Induction is not a one-day event. It normally is a process that continues for several days or weeks.

Think how long it took for you to become comfortable in you job. Chances are it took several weeks to feel in command of your job responsibilities and even longer to understand how your new company operated. You learnt new things continually. It is therefore, not realistic to expect a new employee to be inducted in just a few days, no matter how well you put your plan together.

As previously noted, the first day is critical. Getting the process started on the right foot will ensure the day will be remembered positively. First days are *always* remembered.

If you ask colleagues about their first day, often what you hear will be negative, such as not knowing where to park, which door to enter, finding you boss out of town that day or just being given a bunch of forms to fill out. All these situations can be avoided with planning.

CASE STUDY
Mary's induction

Mary showed up for work bright and early on her first day. After a few introductions, she was told by her new boss to go to a nearby office supply store and buy herself a desk and some supplies. She was instructed to have it delivered by 2 pm.

Mary's boss gave her the name of the office supply store, but no information on what to buy or how much to spend.

She found the store, selected and purchased a desk that was delivered at exactly 2 pm. Somehow the cost of the desk was within the unknown budget.

Mary's first official act was a success, and she subsequently became a valued employee. Many new employees faced with a similar assignment would not be as resourceful as Mary because of the ambiguity. Mary's boss was lucky because Mary could have spent a small fortune or else walked away from a company that was so loosely run.

If you were Mary — what would your reaction have been?

_____

_____

_____

_____

_____

_____

The first day in the job

As you plan your induction programme, strive to make the first day memorable in a positive way. Get things started correctly. When this happens, the rest of the induction will be more effective and go smoother.

One mistake to avoid is trying to cram everything the new employee needs to know into the first day. Schedule the induction over several days. Give each employee enough time to assimilate new information in a way that is meaningful.

New employees are nervous on the first day. This may make it difficult for them to remember everything if you try to cover too much information too soon.

One suggestion is to provide written information, such as an employee handbook containing basic information that can be referred to later. Take time to go over critical items in any written information and encourage questions.

Your first day in the job

Your experience can be an excellent source of ideas on what to do and what _not_ to do on the first day. Think back to the induction you received on the first day in your present job and list the good and not so good things you remember.

Good	_Not so good_
_____	_____
_____	_____
_____	_____
_____	_____

For each item in the 'not so good' column, describe below how you plan to ensure your new employee receives a good experience in that area. Be sure to remember all the 'good' things you experienced and repeat them.

1. _____

_____

2. _____

_____

3. _____

_____

4. _____

_____

5. _____

_____

How to have a successful new employee induction

Your role as a supervisor
Once a job has been accepted and a starting date has been agreed on, the first thing to do is clear your schedule. Induction is not a time to be out of town or locked up in meetings.

As a supervisor, you are responsible for getting things started during induction. It is not the responsibility of a secretary or another employee to do your job. They may be involved, but the new employee should not be assigned to anyone until you have made the initial contact and established a plan for the day.

Make time to meet
A breakfast meeting is a unique way to welcome the

employee. Properly planned, breakfast will allow you to meet in a relaxed setting where you can provide an overview of what the day will hold.

Be on time. If you are late for your first meeting, you will communicate that being on time is not important. Do everything you can to put the employee at ease.

You set the example for everything that happens on the first day. What you do or don't do, what you say or don't say, will be noticed and remembered. The standards you demonstrate will be quickly communicated by your actions.

Your role during induction must be an active one. Devote as much time as possible on the first day to the new employee.

Avoid interruptions
Your initial meeting should be arranged in a place and at a time that avoids interruptions. This will allow you to devote full attention to the employee.

We are all individuals and want to be treated as such. New employees should be made to feel as if they are the most important people you have to see. They should never feel like an interruption to busy schedules. As you meet with each new employee, avoid looking at your watch or talking about all you have to do.

Allow enough time so you won't have to hurry through things. Spending quality time with the new employee will pay dividends in the future.

Staff induction
Induction will include the other parts of an organization. A new employee needs a good overview of how things work and where basic responsibilities lay. A good way to do this is with an overview session which includes representatives from key departments.

This will give new employees the opportunity to meet people outside of their immediate work group. It also provides different perspectives about the organization's products, services and/or goals. The objective is for each new employee to develop an appreciation about how the organization functions.

To make such meetings productive, new employees should be encouraged to develop a list of questions to ask each group that is represented. You may wish to provide a list of suggested questions to ensure each employee's induction time is focused. A prepared list of questions will make it easier for new employees to participate in the meetings.

Some sample questions include:

- What is the responsibility of your department?
- To whom do you report?
- Who reports to you?
- With which departments do you most frequently interact?
- What major projects are currently involving you?
- What are barriers you face in getting your job done?
- What type of interaction do you have with my new department?
- Will we be meeting again?

The best time to schedule staff overview meetings is after an employee has worked a few days. By then that person will know more about the company and be in a better position to ask pertinent questions.

Consider asking a key executive (such as the president) to provide the final overview of the organization's goals and an informal 'state of the state' report. This can be a great way to provide a real feeling of importance for new employees.

Company history

Normally it is a good idea to provide more background on how the company got started, significant events in the company's development (ie when an important product was launched; how the organization decided to diversify, etc). Company history, traditions and culture should be presented in a positive manner.

The goal is to give new employees a sense of identity with the organization. How did it get to where it is today? Who were the founders? What has the growth been like? What is the mission of the organization? Each new employee should have a sense of how the past paved the way for what is happening today.

New employees should feel a sense of pride about past accomplishments. Well presented, a company history will reinforce the decision that joining your company was the best possible choice.

Some large organizations have slide shows or videos available to present the company's story. Be sure any session emphasizes how new employees fit into the future plans of the company. Let each employee feel like part of the future growth.

The organization's history

The history of an organization should provide a new employee with a sense of pride in being selected to join the team. The message should be positive and upbeat. The following worksheet can help you prepare your organization's story.

Parent company (if applicable) _____

_____

Official company name _____

What the name represents _____

Organizational mission _____

_____

Company philosophy _____

_____

Notable achievements _____

_____

Date founded _____

Founders _____

Company size originally _____

Company size now _____

Original products/services _____

_____

Current products/services _____

_____

Recent accomplishments _____

_____

Goals for the future _____

_____

Tour the workplace

Shortly after starting work the new employee should be given a tour of the workplace. During the interview the job candidate may have received a glimpse of the work area. Now is the time to provide an insider's view. Your objective during the tour is to develop a feeling of being part of a team.

During the tour, be sure to spend time where other members of the new employee's team are located. Take time to introduce the new employee to each person. Some friendly 'personalizing' comments (ie 'Sandy is our company volleyball captain.') help to break the ice.

It is a good idea to let others know approximately what

time you will be starting your tour. This way they make it a point to be available for an introduction.

The tour should include the entire facility. Briefly visit each major area and explain how to gain access to the area when necessary. Companies with large facilities sometimes prepare a map for new employees that specifies the correct parking space, entrance, etc.

Don't overlook any area that relates to the new employee's job. Remember, the sooner the new employee knows where things are and how they work, the sooner that person will be productive.

Many new employees unnecessarily have to ask people they don't know where to find the toilets, a copy machine, or the canteen. Use a tour guide worksheet similar to the one in the next section to make sure you properly plan your tour of the workplace.

Tour guide worksheet

Check off each item you need to include on your tour of the workplace. Add any others not on the list.

● Office area	☐ ● Conference room	☐
● Co-workers	☐ ● Canteen	☐
● Secretary	☐ ● Executive offices	☐
● Map of building	☐ ● Restricted areas	☐
● Stairs	☐ ● Copy machine	☐
● Lifts	☐ ● Supply area	☐
● Fire exits	☐ ● Receptionist	☐
● Postroom	☐ ● Word processing centre	☐
● Vending machine	☐ ● Files	☐
● Toilets	☐ ● Staffroom	☐
● Car park	☐ ● Storage	☐

_____   _____

_____   _____

_____   _____

Complete paperwork

Sometimes on the first day it is important to have the new employee complete the necessary paperwork for payroll, life insurance and other items. This is the time to make sure all loose ends are completed. If an employee application is not on file, get one processed. If the employee needs an ID card or a key to gain access to the building, have one available.

Although these paperwork items may seem trivial, they can cause real problems later if not taken care of now. Otherwise it may be necessary to explain why the employee's first wage cheque is late or why family members fail to receive insurance benefits.

If there are some paperwork items that can be completed later, they can be given to the employee along with specific deadlines for completion. Items such as association memberships or the circulation list for periodicals can wait until the employee gets settled in the job.

Job description/organization chart

Also during the first day, arrange a meeting where the new employee receives a copy of his or her job description. Take time to answer any questions the employee has.

Carefully review the purpose of the job description, namely:

- describes what is expected of you by the company
- clearly defines responsibilities
- helps focus on priorities
- helps define what training is needed to do the job
- provides a way by which to evaluate job performance.

Be sure the employee understands clearly the specific duties and responsibilities of the job and what is expected.

A complete job description will describe how the employee's duties contribute to the success of the department and the company.

A copy of the company and department organization chart

should also be provided which explains how the new employee's work group fits into the total organizational structure. This chart should clearly define responsibilities and assignments so employees can see at a glance where their job fits and what the working relationships are among the various departments.

Assign a task

Many supervisors make the mistake of not involving a new employee with some actual work on the first day. Often, instead of being given meaningful work, new employees are handed stacks of papers and manuals to read which will 'acquaint' them with the job. More likely the result will be boredom. Instead of being challenged an employee can quickly become disillusioned if given nothing but busy work.

New employees are eager to demonstrate their skills. Wise managers take advantage of this situation and get the employee actively involved in current projects as soon as possible.

An early assignment that provides a sense of achievement is a great idea, especially if it is followed up later with words of encouragement. Make it a point to acknowledge what the employee has done. Pay attention to the results and comment on them. This increases the likelihood that the employee will continue to work at the same high level in the future.

Since a new employee wants to make a good first impression, make every effort to provide the opportunity to allow the new employee to show his or her stuff.

Take to lunch

If your induction was designed to cover the objectives outlined in this section, a new employee may feel over-whelmed by lunch-time. He or she will be ready for a break and an opportunity to reflect on what has been covered. It is an excellent time to provide answers to any questions resulting from the activities of the morning.

Make every attempt on the first day not to leave the new employee alone at lunch-time. If you cannot be present, then make sure someone has been assigned to take the employee to lunch. It's a nice gesture if the company buys lunch on the first day.

If you weren't able to meet the employee for breakfast, lunch is a good second choice. You may consider inviting selected co-workers to establish the feeling of teamwork. Lunch should be as positive and relaxed as possible. Also it should be on the premises whenever possible. This will help familiarize the new employee with the location and operation of the food service.

Operations induction

If your new employee will be in a staff support function, he or she will need to understand the operational side of the business and should spend a minimum of two days observing how the business operates. The manager you select should represent a good role model for the company.

During this time the employee should be informed firsthand how the projects he or she will be working on will impact the operation of the business. For example, if the new employee is in marketing, assign an operations manager working on the marketing project.

This experience can be a disaster if the manager selected is not capable of communicating a positive image of the company. Like all other facets of your plan, the operations induction must be planned and not just allowed to happen.

A positive experience can be assured if the induction plan makes it clear what is to be accomplished. Take time to review the objectives before a new employee is assigned to a project as an observer. Use the operations induction planning guide in the next section to make sure you have clearly defined your expectations.

Operations induction planning guide

Day: _____

Time: _____

Manager assigned: _____

Objectives to be accomplished:

_____

_____

_____

Activities to be observed:

_____

_____

_____

_____

Sample questions to discuss:

1. How does this activity affect my department?
2. What does my department do well? How could it improve?
3. What do you do when there is a problem with something my department has done?
4. What needs to be done to improve the working relationship between my department and your operation?
5. Was everything accomplished that you planned to achieve?

Closing the day

The way the first day ends is just as important as the way it began. On the way home the new employee will reflect on what took place. Closing on a positive note will give the employee a good feeling. The objective is to do everything possible to ensure the new employee looks forward to returning to work the next day.

Before leaving on the first day, a manager should spend some private time with the employee. Assuming a good effort was put into the first day by the employee, communicate directly that you noticed what was accomplished. Review any progress made on any first work assignment. Find something positive to say about it.

End on a positive note, the same way you would when a guest leaves your home. Walk the employee to the door and do your best to make a good parting impression.

Induction process

New employee induction is a process. To this point, considerable emphasis has to be placed on the first day activities because they are critical. However, the induction process will continue over several days or weeks.

An employee cannot learn everything the first day. In your effort to make the new person feel welcome, limit how much information is communicated. It is better to spread the important information over several days than to cover everything at once. Having a written plan will help keep you on track.

The sample induction plan in the following section will help put together the pieces that have been discussed. Use it along with the checklists, and the induction template (page 69) and you will deliver a quality programme.

Sample induction plan

Week one
Induction to company policies and procedures (days 1–2)
Day one:
- meet with employee (breakfast if possible)
- provide company history
- tour building, explain parking, building security

- introduce to co-workers, show work area
- distribute required paperwork
- provide and/or explain system for office supplies
- provide and discuss job description
- distribute operations manual (if any)

Review policies and procedures:
- normal working hours
- pay days/salary
- incentive plan (if any)
- performance review policies
- new employee probation period
- holidays
- sick leave
- other benefits
- dress/appearance code (if any)
- telephone procedures
- employee discounts
- lunch facilities
- review operations training plan/assignments
- make first job assignment

It is recommended that the balance of day one and most of day two be spent on the first job assignment.

Operations induction (days 3–4)
- work opening shift
  employee shadows management and performs assigned tasks under supervision
- work closing shift
  employee shadows management and performs assigned tasks under supervision

Review/job assignments (day 5)
- write a short report on operations experience. Include observations, suggestions, and questions
- continue work on first job assignment
- receive additional job assignments

- review staff induction schedule

Week two
Induction to staff functions (days 6–10)
- schedule meeting with staff members to discuss functions, organization and interface with the new employee
- staff members to be selected by the employee's manager
- written schedule to be developed and sent to all who will be meeting with the new employee
- employee should have a prepared list of questions to ensure quality of meeting time

Supervisor follow-up (days 1–10)
- supervisor should meet regularly with the new employee during the first two weeks to answer questions and ensure that everything is going according to plan

Monday

9.00–9.45	Roland Jackson	Account Manager
11.00–11.45	Janice Wilson	Advertising Coordinator
1.30–2.00	Bob Simpson	Finance Department
3.00–3.45	Russel Miller	Operations Director
4.45–5.00	Meet with supervisor	

Tuesday

9.00–9.45	Parker Johnson	Research and Development
10.30–11.00	Cheryl Fontaine	Purchasing
12.00–1.00	Lunch with Susan Carson, Personnel Manager	
3.00–3.30	Sam Nordick	Legal Department
4.45–5.00	Meet with Supervisor	

Note: A copy of the induction schedule would be sent to each person on the list, highlighting the scheduled meeting time.

Meetings can be spread over as many days as necessary. No more than four meetings should be scheduled on one day. This permits the employee to work on the first job assignment and not to be overwhelmed by meeting a lot of new people.

CHAPTER 4

Induction for Part-time Workers

Do you need a fast-track induction programme?

Answer each question below (circle either Y (yes) or N (no)). If you answer 'yes' to any question, you should consider developing a fast-track induction for part-time workers as part of your company's overall induction programme.

1. Does your annualized employee turnover exceed 75 per cent?   Y N
2. Do you rely on seasonal part-time help (ie, Christmas, summer)?   Y N
3. Does a segment of employees work (by plan) for less than a full year?   Y N
4. Does your organization continually employ, induct and train new workers?   Y N
5. Would regularly scheduled group induction meetings save your organization time?   Y N

If you answered 'yes' to any of the above, a fast-track induction should be considered in addition to any standard programme. The fast-track programme is especially useful for special circumstances or needs that you experience.

Who needs a fast-track induction?

Many organizations routinely employ, induct and train several employees at the same time. This occurs frequently when:

1. high turnover is the norm
2. employees are employed for short, specified periods of time (ie, holidays)
3. the organization is large and always has new people coming on board.

Restaurants and fast-food establishments frequently face this situation. Any business that uses student workers will face employing and training periods at the beginning of the summer and each new school term. Large companies always have staff openings that need to be filled. It is not unusual for some organizations to have a 100 per cent turnover in staff each year.

Retail stores that rely heavily on seasonal business must add many new employees to meet customer demands. These employees have to be inducted and trained in a short period of time.

In situations like the above, a supervisor's time is limited. With many new employees starting at one time, a fast-track programme can induct several employees in a short period of time.

Special problems and opportunities

Induction for employees who may be on board for only a few weeks is just as important as for those who are starting a career. In fact, probably more important because these employees must become productive immediately. Until they have been inducted and provided with some basic training, new employees won't be very productive.

The induction process for fast-track programmes must be squeezed into a short period of time. It is imperative, therefore, to have an organized programme.

A regular induction schedule makes it possible for a new employee to be inducted within a few days after starting. Because time is so critical some companies have a one-day induction on the first day followed immediately by skills training. The employee may later attend a more formal induction meeting scheduled for all new employees.

Fast-track objectives

The objectives for a fast-track induction are the same as for a standard induction.

- provide a welcome
- develop positive perceptions
- confirm job decision
- speed training to make the new employee productive as quickly as possible
- put the employee at ease.

The irony is that you should have the same quality of induction for any employee who may be with you for six weeks, as for one that will be with you for six years. The only difference is that it must be done more quickly.

Large companies that add new employees on a regular basis will benefit from the 'fast-track' concept. A generic programme can be used over and over to cover general information that all employees need to know. Specific items can then be covered by the new employee's supervisor during other periods in the induction process.

This approach builds in flexibility for both the supervisor and the employee and can make the difference between success and failure with a fast-track programme. A programme must take into consideration the supervisor's need for having a productive employee in a short period of time. The supervisor needs a programme that covers the basics quickly and still allows a focus on skills training. In a fast-track environment, a portion of the responsibility for induction is often shifted from the supervisor to others in the organization.

How to do it and what to cover

There are several things you can do to have an effective fast-track induction:

- use a mini-induction package
- prepare a 'canned' overview covering basic information about the organization/job
- conduct group meetings
- share induction responsibilities with other supervisors
- prepare induction hand-out packets.

Each of these items is described in this section as part of a total induction programme. They may be modified as necessary to meet your organization's needs.

Let's take a closer look at each item.

Mini-induction package

A mini-induction package will save considerable time for a supervisor who has several new employees starting together. This package contains the minimum paperwork a new employee needs to complete, which includes:

- form W-4 for withholding
- form 1-9, employment eligibility verification
- employee agreement
- payroll form
- critical policies (ie alcohol, cash handling, etc)
- probation form (if applicable)
- employee handbook (if available).

The objective is for a supervisor to induct the new employee quickly so training can begin. All of the items on the induction checklist shown on page 68 need to be covered, but many can wait until later after the employee has been on the job a few days. For example, company history may be important, but will not be necessary before the employee begins his or her training.

All the necessary paperwork should be placed in a packet that can be handed to the new employee. This preparation will save time since a supervisor won't have to put together a packet every time a new employee starts. As each item is completed it should be put back in the folder and returned to the supervisor.

When the new employee attends the group meeting, the rest of the induction information can be presented.

The checklist in the next section will help you put together a mini-induction package.

The purpose of the mini-induction package is to give the new employee the minimum information necessary to:

1. satisfy government and company regulations, and
2. answer questions that, if unanswered, could slow the employee's productivity.

Some sample items are listed below:

- application form
- W-4 form
- 1-9 form
- employee agreement
- payroll form
- benefit enrolment
- pay days
- probation form
- employee handbook
- dress/uniform code
- critical policies

Add your own but before you put anything in the package, ask 'Could the employee start training without having to worry about this item?' If your answer is 'yes' the item should *not* be included in the mini-induction package. It can wait until later. If you answer 'no', it should be included.

- _____   • _____
- _____   • _____

Prepare a packaged overview

A packaged overview can be developed to induct new employees to the organization and the job. The presentation can be used over and over again, whenever needed.

One approach is to produce an audio-visual presentation that presents a consistent message to all new employees. The format can be cassette/workbook, slide/tape or videotape.

When a new employee is hired, a supervisor arranges to have the programme presented. This saves supervisor time and helps present a professional image of the company to the new employee.

Properly done, a quality packaged programme will allow the company to sell itself to the new employee and help affirm the employee's decision to join your organization. This type of programme should not be 'thrown together'. A well-developed programme should be both motivating and informative. If you organization doesn't have the talent and resources to produce it inside, you may want to consider getting outside help.

Once you have a programme, you will find other uses for it, such as a recruiting tool or as a motivational reminder to current employees.

Some topics that lend themselves to a packaged presentation include:

- mission and philosophy
- company history
- organization structure
- company position in the marketplace
- commitment to service.

The presentation can be enhanced with some brief upbeat remarks by the company president or other key executives.

Appropriate music and visual images can project a quality image of the organization. A packaged programme should last approximately 15–20 minutes. If it is longer it can start to sound self-serving.

Use the checklist in the next section as a guide to develop a packaged programme.

Packaged induction programme planning

Make notes on the outline below of specific items your organization wants to present in a packaged programme.

1. mission statement
   (a) introduction by president and chief executive officer
   (b) business philosophy
2. Our organization
   (a) who we are
   (b) what we do
3. Major products and commitment to the customer
4. Company history
5. What you can expect as an employee of this organization
   (a) employee success stories
   (b) employee testimonials
6. Future outlook
   (a) new products
   (b) new locations
   (c) new jobs

Conduct group meetings

Group meetings should cover basic information. This will save considerable time. For example, one two-hour meeting with 10 employees, rather than 10 two-hour individual meetings, will save 18 hours.

A successful meeting requires planning. The person conducting it must be comfortable in front of a group. This section will provide guidelines for planning the meeting.

A successful meeting starts with an *agenda* geared to meet your objectives. This agenda should list key activities that will be covered during the meeting and be designed to:

1. keep you on track
2. let the meeting participants know what to expect.

It should include the names and titles of those who will making presentations. This will help new employees associate names, faces and job titles.

In most cases, the preliminary meeting should not last more than two hours. During this time most basics should be covered.

If you use the mini-induction package described earlier, the meeting can answer questions about items an employee has already experienced on the job. It also allows extra time for other items you feel are critical.

The checklist on page 68 can help set an agenda which will answer the questions – who, what, when and where? Refer to the sample agenda for details. Several items covered in the meeting can be reinforced with induction hand-out packets. The development of these packets will be discussed later in the section under 'induction handbook'.

A sample induction meeting agenda

Tuesday 1 March – Main conference room		
8.00–8.20	Welcome/introductions/ purpose	Bob Smith Operations Manager
8.20–8.40	Company history	Bob Smith
8.40–9.00	Company operations	Cindy Parks Operations Vice President
9.00–9.20	Employee benefits	Dan Sellers Benefits
9.20–9.30	Break	

9.30–10.00	Paperwork/questions and answers	Bob Smith
10.00	Adjourn for tour of the workplace	

Arrange a meeting place

Once you have an agenda, the next step is to arrange the *meeting place*. If practical, hold it in a nicely appointed conference area (such as a boardroom). This will give the message that you consider the new employees to be 'special' and have taken extra steps to meet their needs.

The set-up of the meeting room can also contribute to the success of the induction. The best is one in which all attendees can see each other. This creates a sense of togetherness and encourages people to get to know each other.

If possible, you might consider a horseshoe or U-shape arrangement. The presenter can easily see all participants and make frequent eye contact. This set-up also makes distribution of materials easier. Figure 4.1 illustrates what a typical set-up would look like:

Figure 4.1 *A U-shape seating arrangement*

If you are not able to use the U-shape, consider the hollow square or conference style. This simply fills the opening and allows for a few more seats.

Figure 4.2   *Hollow square or conference seating style*

If this won't work, use the traditional classroom format. The major drawback here is that people will be looking over the backs of heads. It is difficult for the participants to see the others without turning round or straining. Sometimes, however, when the group is large, this is the only choice.

Figure 4.3   *Traditional classroom seating format*

It is important to have the tables available or chairs with arms that allow writing. This gives participants room to place materials, take notes or fill out paperwork.

Once the agenda is set and the meeting place is determined, the details should be communicated to those who will be attending.

Whenever possible a written notice is best. The ensures a consistent message (time, date, location, etc) is received by all who attend. It does not, however, ensure everyone will read it. Some companies have found that a telephone confirmation follow-up will help ensure participants who plan to attend know the specifics about the meeting.

Share responsibility for the presentation

When planning the meeting, assignments should be provided to others who will be involved. This is important when you have employees who will be working with different managers or supervisors.

Be sure to prepare each presenter for what you want him or her to accomplish in the meeting. A rehearsal of the presentation is recommended. This way you will know what each person plans to say and how long the presentation will take. Rehearsal allows you to eliminate duplication or add material that might otherwise not be covered. Getting everyone involved will make the meeting more interesting and reduce your workload.

Have a written plan

Start by making a list of items on the agenda to be presented. Assign presenters a topic about which they are knowledge-able. This is best when you have a short time to prepare for the meeting and the presenters are the subject matter experts. For example, a representative from personnel should discuss the benefits programme whenever possible.

Remember, a major objective of induction is to develop positive perceptions. One disorganized presentation can offset the other good things you do during the meeting. Don't skimp on the preparation – it will be evident to all who attend if you are well organized.

Prepare induction packets

Much of what you need for one new employee will be repeated for every new employee. Use the induction checklists and template provided to determine what materials would be effective hand-outs at your induction meetings.

Develop a packet that can be given to each person at an appropriate time during the meeting. You may want to duplicate some items that are included in the mini-induction package. Use the meeting to review the contents of the packet with the participants.

The packet should be as easy to handle as possible. A recommended approach is to use a *file folder packet*. Prepare a file folder for each person to be inducted. Insert all the information in the sequence you want it to be read.

During the meeting it might be appropriate for employees to complete required paperwork. Once completed, the paperwork can be placed back in the file folder. Rather than spending time during the meeting collecting papers, or afterwards collating forms into individual folders, you can have a completed file folder for each employee. Having employees complete forms at the same time encourages them to fill in the information accurately and completely. They can ask questions that may benefit the group if something is unclear.

Induction handbook

A variation on the file folder packet is to insert an induction handbook inside the file folder. This handbook should contain all the forms the new employee needs to complete. Place these in a three-ring binder so they can easily be removed. Setting up a handbook in this manner will save time.

At the appropriate time during the meeting, you can distribute the file folder and induction handbook. When the forms are completed, they can be removed from the handbook and placed in individual file folders.

Regardless of which method you use, the goal is to make the induction process go smoothly and take care of the administrative details for new employees.

By developing each component described in this section:

- mini-induction package;
- packaged overview programme;
- group meetings;
- shared induction responsibilities, and
- induction hand-out packets,

you will have a well-organized and professional fast-track induction programme.

CASE STUDY
Fast-track or off track?

Joe Sherman, a senior student at Woodware High School, decided to enter the world of work. He was hired as a cook at Bob's Better Burgers and told to report on Monday, two hours before the restaurant opened.

When Joe arrived he was greeted by Bob, who handed him a packet of forms. Joe was asked to fill out the forms and put them back in the packet. Joe was directed to a seat in the dining room where two other new employees were already filling out forms.

Joe had a question about one form so he asked one of the new employees about it, since Bob was out of the room. Together the new employees decided the best way to fill in the form. A few minutes later two more new employees arrived and were told to start on their packets. As they sat down, Bob took the first two employees into a corner to show them a videotape about the parent company. Joe worked on the rest of his paperwork, while ignoring the noise from the video.

When the video ended, the first two employees were taken to the kitchen. Joe was then told to watch the video. Next, Joe was taken to the kitchen and trained on operating the French fries machine. The two new employees who were ahead of him had finished their French fry training and were learning about the grill.

Evaluate Bob's induction techniques.

What things were good? _____

_____

What things could be improved? _____

_____

What do you think Joe Sherman's impression was of his first

day on the job?_____

_____

Summary

A fast-track induction process allows several new employees to start together and learn about their new organization in a consistent manner.

Fast-track induction is not a substitute for a thorough process that takes place over several days or weeks. It can be used to get the ball rolling and should be considered as the first phase of a more complete induction process for permanent employees.

During fast-track induction essential information is covered and the stage is set for things such as operations induction. Giving the first job assignment and reviewing the job description are other examples of tasks that may not lend themselves to the fast-track induction process.

Fast-track induction can help get a new employee productive quickly when used in conjunction with the rest of your induction plan. This will save a supervisor time, benefit the employee, the organization and ultimately the customer.

Self-assessment

The following items summarize the key points covered in this chapter. Check the appropriate space.

	Have available	Should modify	Need to develop
Mini-induction package	_____	_____	_____
Packaged overview	_____	_____	_____
Group meetings	_____	_____	_____
● agenda	_____	_____	_____
● meeting place	_____	_____	_____
● assigned presenters	_____	_____	_____
● written plan	_____	_____	_____
Induction hand-out packets	_____	_____	_____

Other items:

_____	_____	_____	_____
_____	_____	_____	_____
_____	_____	_____	_____

Review this list prior to you next major need for employing, induction and training. For example, if you take on Christmas help on 15 November, review you fast-track induction in September. That will give you time to update existing materials and start development of others you need.

CHAPTER 5
Putting it All Together

Introduction

Effective new employee induction requires planning, execution and follow-up. By following the steps in the book, you should have completed an evaluation of your existing programme and identified areas for improvement.

As a final check, review the induction checklists in the next section to make sure you have identified all the pieces you need to develop.

Use the induction template to develop your own specific new employee induction *plan*.

Once developed you will be ready to put it into practice – *execute*.

Then you need to *follow up* regularly to see that it is working as you intended.

This cycle of plan, execute and follow-up, should continue until the programme meets the objectives you set on page 11.

Induction checklist

The items listed below are the most common that should be covered during new employee induction.

The items are listed in three categories. You may wish to define your own categories. The important thing is to have a comprehensive list and to cover all the items.

New Employee Induction

Administrative
- Employment application ☐
- Employee benefits ☐
- W-4 form ☐
- Non-compete agreement ☐
- Insurance forms ☐
- _____ ☐

Personal
- Work area ☐
- Building tour ☐
- Introduction to
  co-workers ☐
- Parking ☐
- Time off ☐
- Vacations/holidays ☐
- Dress/appearance/
  uniforms ☐
- Mail ☐
- Probation period ☐
- Sick pay ☐
- Telephone procedures ☐
- Employee discounts ☐
- Personal use of
  equipment ☐
- _____ ☐

Business
- Job description ☐
- Organization chart ☐
- Hours/work schedule ☐
- Pay rate/pay days ☐
- Incentive plan ☐
- Operations manuals ☐
- Operations induction ☐
- Company policies ☐
- Confidentiality ☐
- Company history ☐
- Office supplies ☐
- Company publications ☐
- Employee handbook ☐
- ID card ☐
- _____ ☐

Miscellaneous
- Recreation activities ☐
- Local items of interest ☐
- _____ ☐

Have you prepared for the new employee's arrival by:

- preparing a written induction plan? ☐
- designating a work area (office, desk, etc)? ☐
- assigning a phone number? ☐
- arranging for office supplies? ☐
- preparing required paperwork and forms for
  completion? ☐
- keeping your schedule free to meet with the new
  employee? ☐

- arranging for lunch the first day? ☐
- scheduling staff induction meetings? ☐
- scheduling an operations induction? ☐
- providing a welcoming get together? ☐
- preparing first job assignment? ☐
- making available copies of appropriate company manuals and publications? ☐

What specifically will you do to:

Provide a welcome?   *Develop positive perceptions?*

_____   _____

_____   _____

Confirm job decision?   *Speed training?*

_____   _____

_____   _____

Put employee at ease?   *Other?*

_____   _____

_____   _____

Induction template

Use this template to create your own individual induction plan.

_____   _____
(Employee)   (Job title)

_____   _____
(Supervisor)   (Start date)

1. Preparation

- Publicity about employee ☐
- Office supplies ☐
- Quiet place to meet ☐
- Arrangements for lunch ☐
- Designated work area ☐
- Paperwork and forms ☐
- Welcoming get-together ☐

2. Activities

Administrative

- _____ ☐
- _____ ☐
- _____ ☐
- _____ ☐
- _____ ☐
- _____ ☐
- _____ ☐
- _____ ☐

Personal

- _____ ☐
- _____ ☐
- _____ ☐
- _____ ☐
- _____ ☐
- _____ ☐
- _____ ☐
- _____ ☐

Business

- _____ ☐
- _____ ☐
- _____ ☐
- _____ ☐
- _____ ☐
- _____ ☐
- _____ ☐
- _____ ☐

Miscellaneous

- _____ ☐
- _____ ☐
- _____ ☐
- _____ ☐
- _____ ☐
- _____ ☐
- _____ ☐
- _____ ☐

3. Operations induction

Day/date   Hours   *Manager*

_____   _____   _____

Activities to be accomplished:

_____

_____

_____

Day/date   Hours   *Manager*

_____   _____   _____

Activities to be accomplished:

_____

_____

_____

4. Staff induction

Day/date:_____

Time   Person   *Title/department*

_____   _____   _____

_____   _____   _____

_____   _____   _____

_____   _____   _____

New Employee Induction

Day/date:_____

Time	Person	Title/department
_____	_____	_____
_____	_____	_____
_____	_____	_____
_____	_____	_____

Day/date:_____

Time	Person	Title/department
_____	_____	_____
_____	_____	_____
_____	_____	_____

Day/date:_____

Time	Person	Title/department
_____	_____	_____
_____	_____	_____
_____	_____	_____

Notes

New Employee Induction

New Employee Induction

New Employee Induction

New Employee Induction